THEMATIC UNIT

INDUSTRIAL REVOLUTION

Written By David Jefferies

Illustrated by Cheryl Buhler

Teacher Created Materials, Inc.
6421 Industry Way
Westminster, CA 92683
www.teachercreated.com

©1993 Teacher Created Materials, Inc.
Reprinted, 2000

Made in U.S.A.

ISBN-1-55734-294-6

Table of Contents

Introduction

The Industrial Revolution was a time of breathtaking technological changes and tremendous social upheaval. It was a time that enriched many but impoverished many more. It was a time when the United States changed from a rural country with few cities and more manufacturing along the rivers of New England to the largest producer of manufactured goods in the world. This unit is centered on two selections that show how young adults actively participated in industry in the United States, both in the work itself and in the labor movement that sought to improve the lives of workers in factories and mines. This unit is rich in opportunities for students to research the period, to learn about it through debate and role play, through games and active experimentation, through poetry, music, and art. In the culminating activity, teams of students will design and develop their own inventions.

This thematic unit includes:

☐ **literature selections** — summaries of two books and reproducible pages that support and expand upon concepts contained in the books.

☐ **planning guides** — suggestions for pacing and organizing the unit.

☐ **writing ideas** — a wealth of ways for students to develop their writing skills as they learn about this historical period.

☐ **poetry** — suggestions about how to integrate poetry of the period into the unit.

☐ **curriculum connections** — in language arts, math, science, social studies, music, art, and cooking.

☐ **map unit** — to work on map skills in a way that will extend the material in the rest of the book.

☐ **group project** — to foster cooperation and social skills.

☐ **bibliography** — suggesting additional books relating to the theme.

☐ **culminating activity** — which requires students to synthesize their learning and produce products that can be shared with others.

To keep this valuable resource intact so that it can be used year after year, you may wish to punch holes in the pages and store them in a three-ring binder.

Lyddie

by Katherine Paterson

Summary

In 1843, Lyddie and her family wait for word from her westward-bound father and try to eke out a living on their small Vermont farm. Lyddie lives on hard work and hope, but she is plunged into a different world when her mother hires her out to a local tavern owner as an indentured servant. Eventually she makes her way to the factories of Lowell, Massachusetts, attracted by the stories of the factory girls and their fine lifestyles. She experiences both the truth and falseness of those stories. She learns about the pains of slavery and the struggles of the early labor movement. The resolution of the story brings Lyddie to the brink of even greater challenges.

The activities that accompany each day's reading were created and organized to coincide with the events of that chapter. Also, optional readings from David Macauley's *The Mill*, Houghton Mifflin Company, 1983 will extend the students' knowledge of water technology in the United States. (See page 22.)

Sample Plan

Day One

- A Little about Vermont (page 9)
- A Personal Time Line (page 10)
- *Lyddie* (Chapters 1&2)
- Begin Double Entry Journal. (pages 7 and 8)
- What Could This Be? (page 12)
- Begin Daily Writing Activities. (page 36)
- Writing Ideas: ("To a Locomotive in Winter") (page 37)

Day Two

- *Lyddie* (Chapters 3-5)
- Double Entry Journal (page 7)
- The Canals of Lowell (page 42)
- Wheels of Power (pages 18 and 19)
- Continue Daily Writing Activities.
- Songs of Labor and Protest (page 65)
- Writing Ideas: (Emily Dickinson and the Train) (page 37)

Day Three

- *Lyddie* (Chapters 6-8)
- Double Entry Journal (page 7)
- Six Vermont Families (pages 13-16)
- Continue Daily Writing Activities.
- Art Ideas: Lyddie's Window (page 64)
- Dickens at the Mills (page 38)

Day Four

- *Lyddie* (Chapters 9-11)
- Double Entry Journal (page 7)
- Building Your Wheel (page 18)
- Continue Daily Writing Activities.
- Writing Ideas: Cubing (page 39)

Day Five

- *Lyddie* (Chapters 12-14)
- Double Entry Journal (page 7)
- In the Boardroom of the Mill (page 52)
- Writing Ideas: (William Cullen Bryant and "The Reapers") (page 37)
- Continue Building Your Wheel.
- Continue Daily Writing Activities.

Sample Plan *(cont.)*

Day Six

- *Lyddie* (Chapters 15-17)
- Double Entry Journal (page 7)
- Testing Your Wheel (page 20)
- Assembly Line vs. the Cottage Industry (page 55)
- Continue Daily Writing Activities.
- A Time Line of Inventions (page 50)
- Writing Ideas: Lyddie's Poem (page 37)
- Compare Homemade and Prepared Cooking. (page 66)

Day Seven

- *Lyddie* (Chapters 18-20)
- Double Entry Journal (page 7)
- Lyddie and Spelling (page 40)
- Art Ideas: B is for Brigid (page 64, continue as necessary)
- Continue Songs of Labor and Protest. (page 65)
- Begin Women of the 1800's Big Book (page 23)

Day Eight

- *Lyddie* (Chapters 21-23)
- Double Entry Journal (page 7)
- On the Railroad (page 41)
- Continue Daily Writing Activities.
- Begin Map Unit (pages 45-49)
- Continue Women of the 1800's Big Book

Overview of Activities

Setting the Stage

1. "A Personal Time Line" (page 10) will allow the students to begin this unit on history with an activity about their own lives.

2. The activities "A Little About Vermont" (page 9) and "What Could This Be?" (page 12) will familiarize students with Vermont and aspects of rural life of the 19th century.

3. Writing Ideas (page 37) will introduce various viewpoints about industry through the medium of poetry. Discussing the advantages and drawbacks of industrialization can be a continuing thread of discussion and debate throughout this unit. Use the poems as models (in either subject or form) for students to write their own.

4. Help students assemble their double entry journals as a method to respond to *Lyddie*.

Enjoying the Book

1. Both the Double Entry Journal and Daily Writing Topics explore the book through writing. The journal asks students questions that engage them directly with the text. The daily topics will help the students connect the incidents and ideas in the book with their own lives or with historical/ social issues.

Overview of Activities *(cont.)*

2. "The Canals of Lowell" (page 42), "The Assembly Line vs. the Cottage Industry" (page 55), and "In the Boardroom of the Mill" (page 52) will widen the students' knowledge about the town of Lowell. Selections from David Macaulay's *The Mill* will give the students another perspective about the events of the book.

3. "Six Vermont Families" (pages 13-16) will help the students understand what happened to Lyddie's family in the context of what has happened in the entire region.

4. "A Time Line of Inventions" (page 50) will ask students to use the idea of the time line developed in "A Personal Time Line" and apply it to the development of ideas and inventions that fueled the Industrial Revolution.

5. "Songs of Labor and Protest" will provide a fuller understanding of the labor and work issues raised in the book. This activity is listed twice for each major selection, but play more music if you find the sources. Whatever songs you find will provide avenues to more reading, writing, and researching activities.

Extending the Book

1. Show students where Oberlin College is (just southwest of Cleveland, Ohio). Introduce "On the Railroad" (page 41). Read about the college in the encyclopedia.

2. Industrial development began in this country along the rivers of the east coast. As settlers spread west, so did the factories. The lessons in the map unit (pages 45-49) will help move the students' focus in the same direction that Lyddie is going at the end of the book.

3. Art Ideas will ask students to do art that is similar to things done in the books. "B is for Brigid" will probably take more than one day to complete.

4. Use the Big Book concept to have students choose a famous woman of the 1800's and research her life. After the Big Book is finished, the class will have a valuable resource.

5. Comparing Homemade and Prepared will compare two ways of cooking. Ask students to compare the modern kitchen with what Lyddie would have used.

Using a Double Entry Journal

There are many advantages to using a double entry journal to explore literary selections. Having the students focus on specific pre-selected passages will help some students respond to the text. Allow students who are more confident about their interpretive skill to respond to a passage of their choice.

Directions

1. Display the selected passage on the board or overhead and have the students copy it onto the left hand side of the journal pages. (Sample passages from *Lyddie* are found below.) Briefly discuss the quote and what it means. (You may choose to do the first exercise together and allow the students to either copy the group's response or write their own.)

2. Allow some time after the writing for students to share their responses. This may be done as a class or in groups of 4-6.

Suggested Passages from *Lyddie*

Lesson 1: *(Chapter 1 "The Bear")*

"She's letting out the field and horse and cow. She's sending you to be the miller's boy and me to housemaid. She's got us body and soul."

Lesson 2: *(Chapter 4 "Frog in a Butter Churn")*

" 'Eyheh,' Triphena continued. 'Some folks are natural born kickers. They can always find a way to turn disaster into butter.' "

Lesson 3: *(Chapter 6 "Ezekial")*

" 'How can you get to Massachusetts? You've no money for coach fare.'

'I'll walk,' she said proudly. 'A person should walk to freedom.'

'A person's feet will get might sore,' muttered Triphena."

Lesson 4: *(Chapter 9 "The Weaving Room")*

"She didn't know how to explain to anyone, that it wasn't so much that she had gotten used to the mill, but she had found a way to escape its grasp. The pasted sheets of poetry of Scripture in the window frames, the geraniums on the sill, those must be some other girl's way, she decided. But hers was a story."

Lesson 5: *(Chapter 14 "Ills and Petitions")*

"She marveled that there had been a time when she had most gladly given to a perfect stranger everything she had, but now found it hard to send her own mother a dollar."

Lesson 6: *(Chapter 15 "Rachel")*

"In her uneasy sleep she saw the bear again, but, suddenly, in the midst of his clumsy thrashing about, he threw off the pot and was transformed, leaping like a spring buck up into the loft where they were huddled. And she could not stare him down."

Lesson 7: *(Chapter 19 "Diana")*

"Everything else that had made her know herself as Lyddie Worthen was gone. Nothing but hard work — so hard that her mind became as calloused as her hands — work alone remained."

Lesson 8: *(Chapter 23 "Vermont, November 1846")*

"To stare down the bear! The bear that she had thought all these years was outside herself, but now, truly, knew was in her own narrow spirit."

Lyddie

Double Entry Journal

Your Name:

My comments and reaction:

Book Title:

Quote from book:

8

A Little About Vermont

Find a map of Vermont in an almanac, atlas, or encyclopedia and answer the following questions:

1. What is the capital of Vermont?

   _____

   Locate it and draw a star on your map. Write in the name.

2. These towns will be mentioned in the book *Lyddie*:

   Burlington, Windsor, Poultney, Rutland, and Ferrisburg. Find and put them on your map.

3. Which three states border Vermont?

   _____ _____ _____

4. Which province of Canada borders Vermont? _____

5. Lyddie's brother, Charles, worked at a mill. The mill might have been on the White River. Find the river and draw it in on your map.

6. Mt. Mansfield is the highest point in Vermont. Find it and draw it in.

   What is its elevation? _____

A Personal Time Line

Begin this unit on history by giving students a sense of their own past and how to record it.

Materials: Copies of page 11, tape, markers

Directions

1. Explain to the students that they are beginning a unit on history. One way to begin that unit is to explore their own history. Introduce the idea of a time line as one way to describe history.

2. Brainstorm a list of the kinds of things students may want to put on their time lines. Make sure such items as birthdays, special trips, moving, changes in the family, and other births and deaths are included.

3. Each time line segment covers two years, so each month is represented by one centimeter. Have students cut one segment to begin with their birth date (e.g., the first segment for a student born in April would be eight centimeters long). Give each student enough to cover his/her whole life.

4. First have the students fill in the proper years. Then have them fill in the incidents in their lives. If they are not sure in which month some of the incidents occured, the students may approximate.

5. Post time lines when they are finished.

Extensions: The students may also do time lines of other members of their families. Or they may do time lines for historical figures of the Industrial Revolution.

Checklist of Dates to Include on Timeline

☐ When were you born?

☐ When did you first talk?

☐ When did you first walk?

☐ When did you learn to:

— tie shoes?

— ride a bike?

— read?

☐ When did you start school?

☐ When did you meet some of your best friends?

☐ Important family events:

— birthdates of sisters, brothers, cousins

— family marriages or divorces

— deaths in the family

☐ Have you moved?

— when?

— where?

Time Line Template

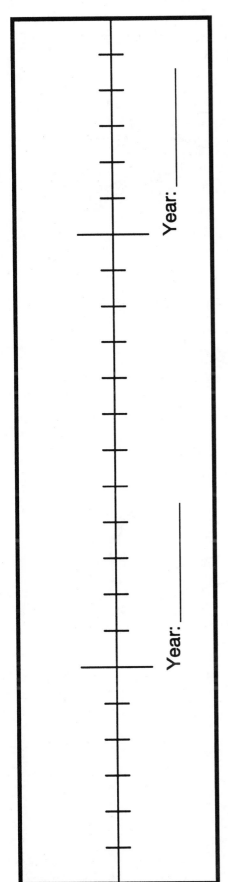

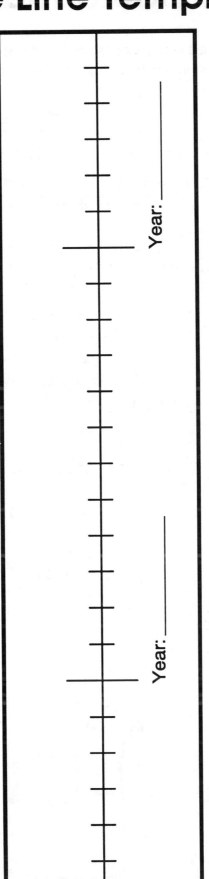

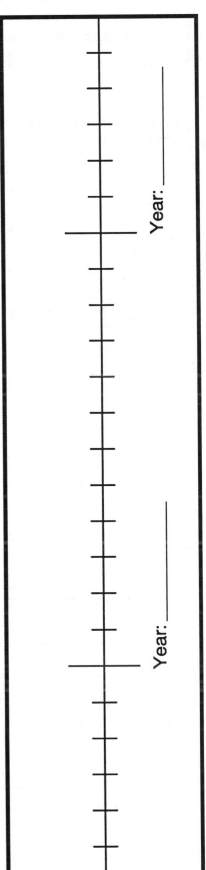

What Could This Be?

Farmers in the early United States used machines to help them do their work faster. Here are pictures of four of them, and some hints to help you. Try to decide what they could have been.

1. This was used in the kitchen. It was turned in front of the fire.

   _____

2. This is another kitchen utensil. People put their hands on the cylindrical part.

   _____

3. This helped feed livestock. It has something to do with corn.

   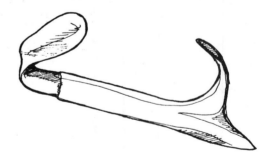

   _____

4. This was used in the house. It used coals to get hot.

   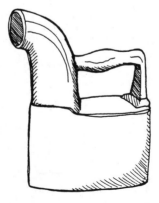

   _____

12

Six Vermont Families

Telling the stories of specific families will help students see the movement of Americans from the country to the city.

Materials: copies of pages 14-16 for each group.

Background: In many ways, the rise of the American city coincides with the rise of American Industry. Waves of immigration fed both of those phenomena. In 1790 only 5.1% of the population of this country lived in urban areas. Through 1830, the cities grew slowly. From 1860 to 1910, the population of the United States rose from 31 million to 91 million. The urban population, however, rose from 6 million to 41 million.

Directions

1. Divide your class into six groups. Explain that they will have the chance to follow a family from the time of the book to the present.

2. Pass out the 1850's slips. Have groups read over the scenarios. Discuss where the family is living, who is working and in what kinds of jobs, who is going to school, who is moving (and where). Who is living in the city? In the country?

3. Continue with the 1900 and 1950 scenarios. The scenarios were written with an eye toward including various important historical events. Any of these events might provide the beginning of research the group might do. Provide a time for them to conduct this research.

4. Give students time to write their own scenarios about the year 2000. Ask groups to focus on the same issues raised in the discussions of 1850-1950.

5. In a group of four, divide responsiblities by having one student in each group be a spokesperson for the four time periods (including the year 2000).

Note: These six families are not representative of all of American society. Many of our ancestors have not been in the country that long. Many immigrants moved directly to the large cities. Discuss how the stories of various ethnic groups might be different. Allow time for students to discuss their own backgrounds.

Extension: The movement of the families might be clearer if you put up one (or several) maps and use them to show the families' progress, using captions and yarn to show movements.

1850

The Stewarts — The Stewarts emigrated from Scotland to run a grain mill on the White River, Vermont. After ten years, they could afford their own mill. But the farmers in the area were all going west and business was getting worse. The Stewart children were lucky enough to be able to go to school.

1900

The Pecks — The Pecks moved to Wyoming to try sheep raising there. When the parents died, one daughter stayed on to keep running the ranch. Other members of the family went west to Oregon and Washington. One son joined the Army and was killed in the Spanish American War.

1950

The Albrights — The daughter who went to college wanted to be a doctor, but few women were admitted to medical school in those days. She became a nurse, but her daughter did go to medical school. She became a doctor in Nashville, Tennessee. One of her sons moved to Seattle, Washington to work for a company that makes planes.

Six Vermont Families *(cont.)*

1850

The Colters — The Colters were raising a variety of crops: corn, wheat, and oats, in the country near Rutland, Vermont. The price they could get for their crops was dropping. One of the daughters went to work in Lowell, Mass. but three years later died of tuberculosis. The Colters had to sell the farm and move west.

1850

The Pecks — In upstate Vermont the Pecks owned a flock of merino sheep. Since 1823 they used the Champlain Canal to get their wool cheaply to the markets in New York City. Now they find that wool from the midwest is cheaper. The Pecks will either switch to raising cows or move west to raise sheep.

1850

The Albrights — The Albrights had three sons and one daughter. In 1837 they had to move from their farm to the manufacturing city of Burlington, Vermont. One son died of pneumonia. The father, one son, and one daughter worked in lumber and cotton mills. The son learned a lot about machines. The family was just getting by.

1850

The Emersons — The Emersons never had much land and what they had was barren and hard to farm. When Mr. Emerson heard about gold in California, he went. Two years later his wife and two sons heard that he had died on the way. The sons are old enough to work in a granite quarry when they aren't farming.

1850

The Stewarts — The Stewarts emigrated from Scotland to run a grain mill on the White River, Vermont. After ten years, they could afford their own mill. But the farmers in the area were all going west and business was getting worse. The Stewart children were lucky enough to be able to go to school.

1850

The Wilsons — The Wilson family could not all live on the farm. The father and one daughter were working in mills in Massachusetts. Another daughter with some education had moved to Ohio and was teaching school. Two sons and the mother are still on the farm, getting money the family sends to them in the mail.

14

Six Vermont Families *(cont.)*

1900

The Colters — The family bought a small farm in Illinois. One son served in the Union Army in the Civil War and stayed in the army after the war. He lived in army posts in Montana. His daughter married a man in Kansas. In 1893 the U.S. violated its treaty with the Native Americans and opened the Oklahoma Territory for settlement. The daughter and her husband began a wheat farm there.

1900

The Pecks — The Pecks moved to Wyoming to try sheep raising there. When the parents died, one daughter stayed on to keep running the ranch. Other members of the family went west to Oregon and Washington. One son joined the Army and was killed in the Spanish American War.

1900

The Albrights — After the parents died, the son moved to Charlotte, North Carolina, because many textile mills moved there. He was skillful with machinery so was made foreman of a mill. He married and had three daughters. One daughter went to college.

1900

The Emersons — When Mrs. Emerson died, the sons had no reason to stay in Vermont. One served in the U.S. Army in the Civil War and died of a disease. The other went to Chicago and got work in a meat-packing plant. He joined the union.

1900

The Stewarts — After having a farm in Illinois for ten years, the children went to live in various cities and small towns in the Midwest. One son moved to Detroit and worked in the Soo Canals on the Great Lakes. A daughter moved to Chicago and was active in the movement to give women the right to vote.

1900

The Wilsons — The daughter who moved to Lowell married and had a daughter who lives in nearby Lawrence and also works in mills. The school teacher in Ohio moved to Cleveland. She still teaches school and her husband works for a steel company. They want their son to go to college.

Six Vermont Families *(cont.)*

1950

The Colters — During the Dust Bowl time in the 1930's, the family lost the farm. Like many Oklahomans they went to California. They had to start over, taking any jobs they could. One boy served in the Marines during World War II. He went to college on the G.I. Bill and lives in Los Angeles working for an insurance company.

1950

The Pecks — The son of the woman who stayed in Wyoming went to college and became interested in farming. He stayed in Wyoming when that state began to use irrigation. Later he moved to California to work on irrigation projects in the San Joaquin Valley. His children now live in San Francisco. One daughter is a lawyer.

1950

The Albrights — The daughter who went to college wanted to be a doctor, but few women were admitted to medical school in those days. She became a nurse, but her daughter did go to medical school. She became a doctor in Nashville, Tennessee. One of her sons moved to Seattle, Washington to work for a company that makes planes.

1950

The Emersons — Some of the family still lives in Chicago. One boy served in the Navy during World War I. During the Depression, he became a reporter for a Chicago newspaper. His daughter moved to Houston, Texas. She works for an oil company.

1950

The Stewarts — Members of the family stayed in Detroit and began working for the car companies there. One granddaughter built cars during World War II when the men were away at war. When the men came back, she lost her job. One of her daughters thought that was very unfair.

1950

The Wilsons — The mill worker in Lawrence was involved in a famous strike in 1912. She continued to work there, but her children left the city before the mills died out. The son in Cleveland did go to college. He became a chemistry professor at Ohio State University.

16

Six Vermont Families *(cont.)*

To the Year 2000

Let's take the family to the year 2000.

1. Where was the _____ family in 1950? What were they doing?
   (family name)

   _____

   _____

   _____

   _____

2. Where will the family be in the year 2000? What will they be doing?

   _____

   _____

   _____

   _____

3. Important historical events occured between the years 1950 and the present. Which ones did the family play a part in?

   _____

   _____

   _____

   _____

4. What jobs do members of the family have?

   _____

   _____

   _____

   _____

Using Wheels of Power

Give your students a chance to learn the basics of water power in a concrete way.

Materials: copies of pages 18-21, stiff paper (like cereal boxes), rulers, scissors, wire hangers or Tinker Toys®, wooden dowels, large tray

Directions

1. Discuss how a water wheel produces energy. Tell the students they will have a chance to make and test their own water wheels.

2. Form construction groups. Distribute Wheels of Power (page 19) and have the groups read it together. Discuss any questions the groups may have.

3. Pass out directions for making the wheel. Make the materials available and have students build their wheels.

4. The template on page 21 is only one of many ways to make a wheel. Encourage experimentation. Groups may wish to modify the existing design, especially groups who have already tested the wheel.

Directions for Building a Wheel

1. Cut out the templates for circle and the blades. Trace two circles and eight blades on stiff paper. Cut them out. Mark the 8 inserts on your cutouts and make a cut where indicated. Make a hole in the center of the circles.

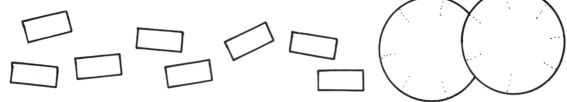

2. Insert the 8 blades into the two circles. Tape the blades onto the circles. Put tape across the blades to protect it against the water. Insert the rod through the center of the circles and tape the rod against the circle.

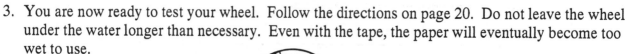

3. You are now ready to test your wheel. Follow the directions on page 20. Do not leave the wheel under the water longer than necessary. Even with the tape, the paper will eventually become too wet to use.

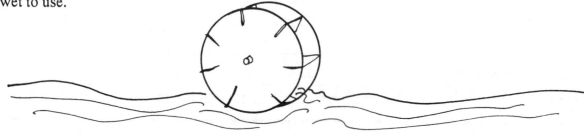

18

Wheels of Power

Beginning industries needed a constant source of power. Gasoline and electric motors had not yet been invented, so manufacturers turned to water power. They used the power generated by falling water to turn a water wheel. They then used gears to use that power to grind wheat or operate a loom. Here are three ways that the water was channeled to turn the wheel.

The Undershot Wheel

Here water flowing under the wheel is used to turn the wheel in counter-clockwise direction.

The Overshot Wheel

Water flows over the wheel and falls into buckets, turning the wheel in a clockwise direction.

The Breast Wheel

Water enters the wheel on the upstream side like the undershot wheel. But it falls into buckets halfway up the wheel, turning it in a counter-clockwise direction.

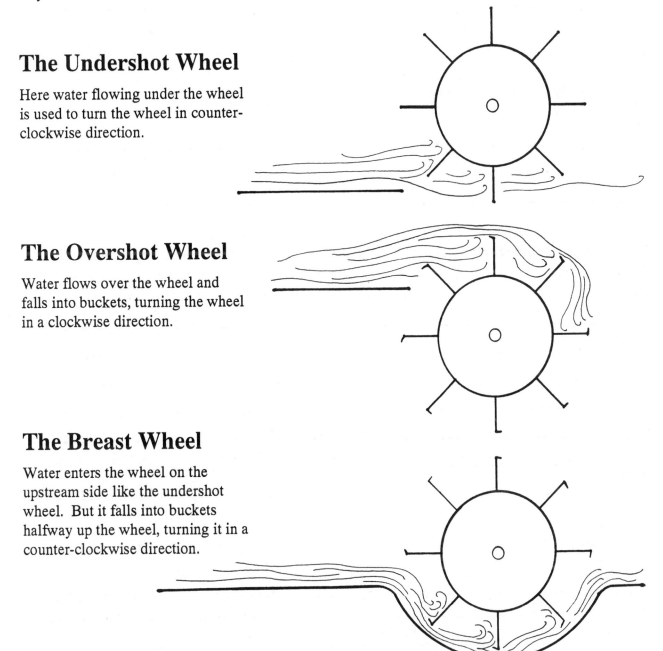

Each of these wheels had advantages and disadvantages. Choosing the right kind of wheel for a particular mill was a decision that could make the mill a success or failure.

Testing Your Wheel

Use two wire hangers to make a stand for your water wheel. Use this picture:

1. Bend hangers so they will stand.

2. Bend hook to form a U to insert
    the axle of the wheel.

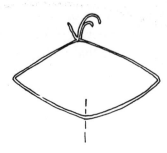

1. Direct a steady stream onto the blades. What happens? Do they move easily?

    _____

    _____

    _____

2. Experiment with different ways of supplying the water. How could you make a breast wheel?
    Explain what you did. Make a picture on the back.

    _____

    _____

    _____

    _____

    _____

    _____

3. How could you redesign this wheel so that it would work better? Think of a few ideas and try one
    out. Write about what happened.

    _____

    _____

    _____

    _____

    _____

Templates for a Water Wheel

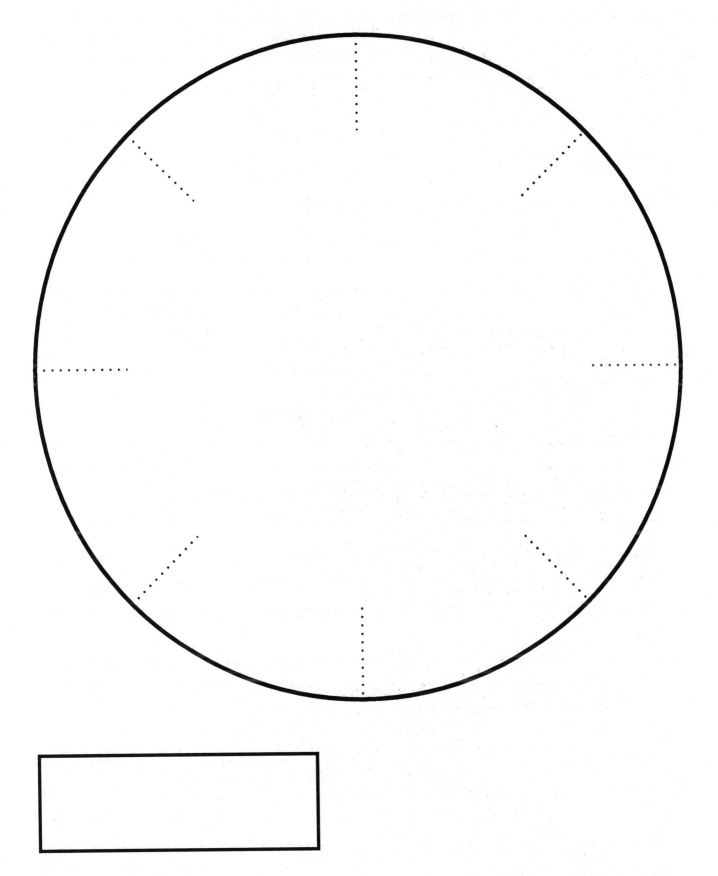

On Macaulay's *Mill*

David Macauley is an author who specializes in showing in the most specific ways how things are actually constructed. In *Mill*, he takes us step by step through the water-driven technology that culminated in the factories of Lowell. This book will give a detailed pictorial sense of the factory where Lyddie worked.

After a brief introduction, Macaulay's book is divided into four sections:

The Yellow Mill:	Circa 1810	pages 14-64
The Stone Mill:	1829	pages 65-88
The Plimpton Mill:	1852	pages 89-106
Harwood Mill:	1870	pages 107-125

The chapter on the Plimpton Mill is the one that is chronologically closest to the events of Lyddie, but any part of the book, or the entire book, will serve as an excellent complement to the action of Lyddie.

Lyddie is primarily interested in the interplay of the characters set against the early industrialization of New England, but the Macaulay book will deal primarily with the technology of the time period. The following are some suggestions about how *Mill* may best be integrated with *Lyddie*:

1. The Introduction and the beginning of "The Yellow Mill" will help students understand the principles of water wheel building. They should be read before or during the students' attempts to construct a water wheel.

2. The last 7-8 pages of "The Yellow Mill" and the end of "The Stone Mill" will provide background about early loom machinery. Those passages might best follow the reading of chapters 9-11.

3. The "Harwood Mill" section describes the construction of a company town. It could be read as a backup to the activity about the canals of Lowell.

Other extensions:

1. Students might use materials to build a replica of a mill, complete with millrace, wooden mill, etc.

2. The problem of how to transmit the rotary energy of the wheel through gears might excite some of the engineers in your class.

3. Macauley has written a series of fascinating books on architecture, including *Cathedral*, *Pyramid*, and *Castle*. Students interested in how things are put together might be motivated by Macauley's other books.

Big Book of Famous Women of the 1800's

The issue of women's rights is central to the action of *Lyddie*. This activity will extend the action of the book by investigating the lives of important women of the 1800's. It will also give students the opportunity to develop their artistic and storytelling abilities.

Materials: encyclopedias, biographies of famous women

Directions

1. The ending of *Lyddie* naturally leads a reader to wonder how the rest of Lyddie's life turned out. Did she go on to get a college education? Did she go back to Vermont? Begin this activity with a discussion of those questions.

2. Turn the discussion to female historical figures. Does the class think that other women who went on to become famous had beginnings like Lyddie's? Were the women born into poor families? Did they have to struggle like Lyddie did to achieve what they wanted? How could the class find out?

3. Briefly introduce some historical figures. Here are some examples:

   - Susan B. Anthony
   - Victoria Woodhull
   - Elizabeth Cady Stanton
   - Emma Goldman
   - Ernestine Rose
   - Sojourner Truth
   - Emily Dickinson
   - Lucretia Mott
   - Margaret Sanger (1900's)

   - Jeanette Parkin
   - Loretta Velasquez
   - Esther Morris
   - Belle Boyd
   - Helen Keller
   - Clara Barton
   - Mary Cassatt
   - Ann Sullivan
   - Harriet Beecher Stowe

4. Organize the class into research teams of 3-4. Have the students research, write and illustrate one woman's life. Have each individual biography make up a chapter in the class's Big Book.

Biographical Research Sheet

1. Name:_____

2. Dates of birth/death:_____

3. Describe the individual's early life._____

   _____

   _____

   _____

   _____

4. Describe the individual's education and career. _____

   _____

   _____

   _____

   _____

5. What was the person's most important contribution? _____

   _____

   _____

   _____

   _____

6. Are the issues this woman confronted still important today? How?

   _____

   _____

   _____

   _____

Breaker

By N.A. Perez

Houghton Mifflin, 1988

Summary

Pat lives in the shadows of the mines in hard coal country in northern Pennsylvania. The book begins with tragedy; his father dies in a mine cave-in. So Pat, age 14, begins his life of work in the mines. He is a breaker (someone who sits all day in the dust and cold picking out the stones from the coal). He learns about the hardships of labor and the tensions among the different ethnic groups in the towns. He learns about the growing efforts to organize the workers into a union and their dreams of better pay and safe working conditions.

Each lesson is intended to supply a full day's curriculum. You may need to tailor the lessons to fit the needs of your class.

Sample Plan

Lesson 1

- Begin Daily Writing Activities. (page 36)
- Read Chapters 1-3 of *Breaker*.
- Begin Double Entry Journal and continue daily as desired. (page 30)
- The State of Pennsylvania (page 28)
- Continue Map Unit. (pages 45-49)
- Begin Culminating Activity (pages 67-78)
- Art Projects: Make a Flag (page 64)

Lesson 2

- Continue Daily Writing Activities.
- Read Chapters 4-6 of *Breaker*.
- Information Hunt on Coal (pages 29)
- Continue Map Unit. (pages 45-49)
- The TV on the Spot Report (page 51)
- Immigration Patterns (page 43)
- Continue Culminating Activity. (pages 67-78)

Lesson 3

- Continue Daily Writing Activities.
- Read Chapters 7-9 of *Breaker*.
- Inventor Concentration (pages 58-61)
- Art Ideas: Charcoal drawings (page 64)
- Continue Culminating Activity.
- Continue Songs of Labor and Protest. (page 65)

Lesson 4

- Continue Daily Writing Activities.
- Read Chapters 10-12 of *Breaker*.
- Making the Grade. (page 44)
- The Industrialists (pages 31-33)
- Continue Culminating Activity.
- Cubing: Group Writing (page 39)

Sample Plan *(cont.)*

Lesson 5

- Continue Daily Writing Activities.
- Read Chapters 13-15 of *Breaker*.
- Writing Ideas: "The Chimney Sweeper" (page 37)
- Philosophical Chairs (pages 62-63)
- Begin Famous Labor Disputes. (pages 34-35)
- Art Ideas: "Another Traffic Signal" (page 64)
- Continue Culminating Activity.

Lesson 6

- Continue Daily Writing Activities.
- Read Chapters 16-18 of *Breaker*.
- Continue Famous Labor Disputes. (pages 34-35)
- Replay Inventor Concentration. (pages 58-61)
- Songs of Labor and Protest (page 65)
- Continue Culminating Activity.

Lesson 7

- Continue Daily Writing Activities.
- Read Chapters 19-21 of *Breaker*.
- Have panel discussion for Famous Labor Disputes. (pages 34-35)
- Writing Ideas: "Southern Pacific" (page 37)
- Finish Culminating Activity

Overview of Activities

Setting the Stage

1. "The State of Pennsylvania" (page 28) will give the students a background about the setting of the book.

2. Gather a few books about coal and mining before you begin this activity. You might use this activity as a way to introduce/review how to use the card catalog in the library.

3. Introduce *Breaker* by discussing the idea of children and work. Ask the following questions: Why don't children work? What jobs could children do? How have the students made money in their lives? Does anyone make money or help his/her family in a business?

Enjoying the Book

1. Three chapters of *Breaker* are scheduled for each day. If you wish to use the double entry journal for this book you will find suggested passages on page 30.

2. The "TV on the Spot Report" (page 51) will supply information about a famous industrial disaster in a way that can be used to report on many other books and historical incidents. Have students research mining disasters and present reports. If possible, get a video recorder and record a report for other classes.

26

Overview of Activities *(cont.)*

3. *Lyddie* happens during a period in which the Irish made up a large proportion of the immigrants. By the time of *Breaker*, much of the immigration came from Eastern Europe. Immigration Patterns (page 43) will give students the sense that immigration to the U.S. has changed over time. If possible, find out which countries are presently sending more immigrants to this country. Make graphs and tables.

4. An abundance of cheap labor helped fuel the industrialization of this country. So did the inventions of the 19th century. "Inventor Concentration" (pages 58-61) will provide an easy way to have students learn about some of the major inventors of the 19th and 20th centuries.

5. Many Pennsylvania coal mines were owned by the railroads. Railroads were important to industrialization in other ways. "Making the Grade" (page 44) gives students experience in some basic physics of railroading.

6. *Breaker* is told from the point of view of the working class. "The Industrialists" (pages 31-33) will give students important information about some of the men who profited by their labors.

Extending the Story

1. Writing Ideas are scheduled throughout this unit. Each one is designed to extend ideas contained in the book.

2. The Industrial Revolution is a controversial period in American history. Some people focus on the advances in science and technology. Other people focus on the terrible human cost in making these advances. Both sides of the question need adequate explanation to help students frame their own judgments. "Philosophical Chairs" (pages 62-63) will give students a structure to participate in that debate.

3. It is important for students to understand that the labor management turmoil of *Breaker* was not an isolated incident. "Famous Labor Disputes" (pages 34-35) will give students important information about other labor disputes of the period.

4. "Make Your Own Invention" (pages 67-78) will take students through the major steps in developing, patenting and marketing a new invention. You might check to see if your community has an inventors' club, and invite a representative to the class to see the class's products. Project Excel (see bibliography) can put you in touch with numerous invention contests.

The State of Pennsylvania

Answer the questions below by finding the information in an almanac, atlas, or encyclopedia.

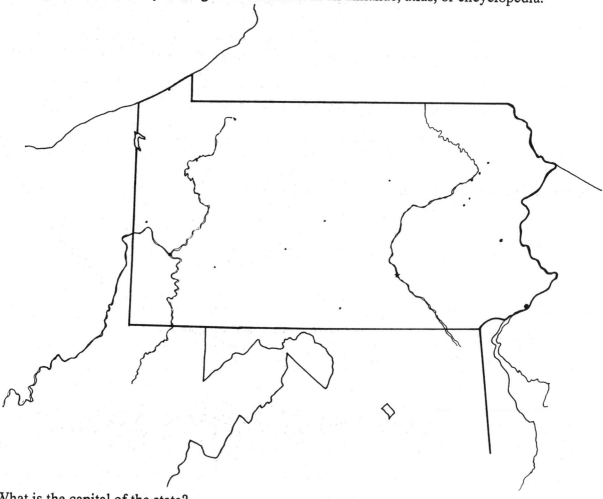

1. What is the capital of the state? _____

    Locate it with a star on the map and write the name.

2. These towns will be mentioned in the book *Breaker*: Pittston, Hazleton, Philadelphia, Freeland, Wilkes-Barre, and Scranton. Find them and draw them on the map.

3. Find out where the anthracite (hard coal) regions of the state are. Color them lightly in green.

4. Find out where the bituminous (soft coal) regions of the state are located. Color them lightly in blue.

5. Pennsylvania has many important rivers, among them the Susquehanna, the Allegheny, the Monongahela, and the Ohio. Find them and trace their paths.

6. Other important cities in Pennsylvania include Pittsburg, Erie, and Allentown. Find them and place them on the map.

7. Where do you think Scatter Patch was? Ask the teacher to reread the first two pages of Chapter Three from the book *Breaker* after you decide.

Information Hunt on Coal

1. Find out how coal is formed. Write a short description.

   _____

   _____

   _____

   _____

2. There are four varieties of coal. Find their names.

   _____   _____

   _____   _____

3. How is coal used in producing steel?

   _____

   _____

   _____

   _____

4. How do we use coal in this country? What problems does its use create?

   _____

   _____

   _____

   _____

   _____

Passages for Double Entry Journal;

For information on how to use a Double Entry Journal see page 7.

Lesson 1: *(Chapter 2)*

"With a queer pang, Pat noticed that she had given him his father's tin bucket, only polished up to look quite bright again."

Lesson 2: *(Chapter 6)*

"Until he had gone to the breaker he had never realized how completely work would fill his life. Free time was precious to him now, and to Annie, too."

Lesson 3: *(Chapter 7) Mr. Foley talking:*

" 'Yet we share one thing in common,'

'We're all poor,' piped Kevin Dugan.

'Yes, but it is coal that connects us. Coal is money, it is power, it is even political.' "

Lesson 4: *(Chapter 12)*

"It was no longer an exciting holiday event, Pat realized, but just an ugly contest to prove one group was better than another."

Lesson 5: *(Chapter 13) Joanna speaking:*

"So you're ashamed of him because he's Polish...and that means that you're ashamed of me."

Lesson 6: *(Chapter 16)*

"Babies came along everyday, heaps of them, and it surprised him that anyone could still get excited over it, think *Maybe this one will make a difference.*"

Lesson 7: *(Chapter 20)*

"Scatter Patch was a poor, drab, ugly place. Hard things happened there. Yet Pat sensed he was connected to it in a way that Cal was not, to the good and the bad, the light and the dark."

The Industrialists

In traditional histories, the life stories of a few men dominated the scene. Who were these men? What did they have in common? How were they different from each other?

This activity assumes you and the students know how to use Venn diagrams. They are good ways to show similarities and differences between two subjects, in this case the biographies of industrialists. Make two interlocking circles on a piece of butcher paper. Label the two circles; this one, for example, is labeled Rockefeller and Ford. In the overlapping portion, the students will write ideas or facts that are true of both men. The non-overlapping portions of the circles are for ideas and facts that are true of only one of the men.

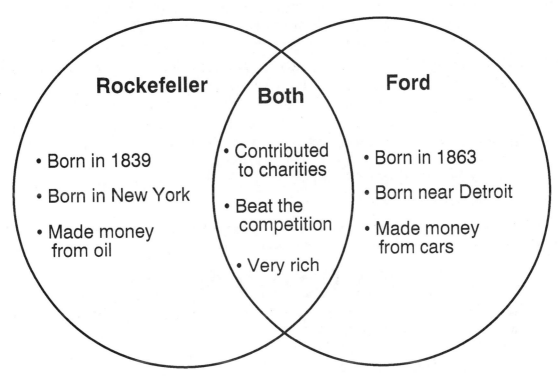

Rockefeller

- Born in 1839
- Born in New York
- Made money from oil

Both

- Contributed to charities
- Beat the competition
- Very rich

Ford

- Born in 1863
- Born near Detroit
- Made money from cars

Materials: copies of pages 32 and 33, large butcher paper for Venn diagram and for questions, encyclopedias, and other reference materials

Directions

1. Divide the class into groups of four; each student in the group of four will become an expert on a separate biography. The students first read their biographies to themselves and then to the rest of the group. Encourage students to find more information using encyclopedias and other resources.

2. Students choose two of the figures and do a Venn diagram for them. They then do a second diagram for the other two men.

3. Students use a third piece of paper to write down questions they have about the men or the industries they helped create. Questions may provide the subjects for further research.

4. Give students time to share their diagrams and questions.

James Jerome Hill

James Hill was born in Ontario in 1838, and at an early age was forced to work. When he was 18, he left home and went to St. Paul, Minnesota. He took a job with a steamship company and later organized his first company, the Red River Transportation Company, after competing with and beating a large company. But he thought there was more promise in the new idea of railroads. He bought a bankrupt railroad and took a daring chance, promising to complete a line within a certain amount of time. He succeeded and was on his way to being both rich and powerful. He added track to his railroad, now called the Great Northern Railway. He waited until his chief competitor, the Northern Pacific, was in financial trouble, and he bought them out. He now had a monopoly on railroads west of the Mississippi River. He also owned steamship lines to the Far East. In the 1900's another industrialist, Averill Harriman, tried to take over his railroad company. After a costly battle, the two men compromised. Hill maintained his wealth and power until his death in 1916.

John Rockefeller

Rockefeller was born in 1839 in New York. He went to high school and got a job as a bookkeeper. He was so good at saving money that in 5 years he went into the grain business. At the age of 23 he became interested in a new industry, oil. There were many small companies competing for oil and its markets. None were organized. Rockefeller built refineries in Cleveland and slowly began to control the oil market in the East. He controlled not only refining but also built his own tankers and barrels. He sought to control everything connected to the oil business, not just the wells.

By 1883 he controlled about 85% of the nation's oil business. Throughout his life, Rockefeller was a great contributor to charities. It is estimated he gave away about $550 million during his life.

Henry Ford

Henry Ford was born in 1863 near Detroit, Michigan. At the age of 16 he got a job with a machinist because he had always been fascinated with machines. In the 1890's he began trying to build a gasoline-powered car. He was not the only one trying to do that. People in Europe and the U.S. had built machines similar to the car. When Ford began building cars for sale in the late 1890's, once again he was not alone. Hundreds of small companies were doing the same thing. Ford became the dominant car maker by using the assembly line process to build his cars. Not only were all his cars the same, he was able to build them so cheaply that owning a car became a possibility for most people in the country. And Ford became rich in the process. He had other interests, too. He sent a peace mission to Europe in 1915; it failed. Later in life he turned over much of the running of the company to his family and devoted himself to making a museum named Greenfield Village. He donated large amounts of money to the Ford Foundation, which still does charitable work.

J.P. Morgan

Morgan was born in 1837 to prosperous parents. His father went on to become a rich banker; and, after Morgan finished two years of college, he became a banker himself. He began to arrange the sales of large companies. Instead of controlling companies with his own money, he used money that other people had invested in his banks to control them. He had so much money under his control that he was twice able to help the U.S. government avoid bankruptcy. He was one of the most powerful men in the country. In 1901 his efforts brought into being the U.S. Steel Company, the most valuable company in the world. Morgan liked spending his money on art works, yachts, and fine champagne. After he died, he willed many of his works of art to the Metropolitan Art Museum of New York City.

Famous Labor Disputes

Long and bitter labor disputes played an important part in how the workers in factories and mines struggled to improve their lives. In this activity students will research a few of the most famous labor disputes.

Materials: copies of page 35, encyclopedias, and books about the labor movement

Directions

1. Divide the class into groups of five. Assign each group one of the following labor disputes: Ludlow Mine Strike, Homestead Steel Strike, Haymarket Riots, Pullman Strike, and the Lawrence Textile Strike.

2. Divide the responsibilities of each group as follows: one recorder to write the material on page 35, one labor expert to research the information about the labor union(s) involved, one management expert to find the information about the company involved, one government expert to research the role of the U.S. government in the strike, and one reporter to report the information gathered and to participate in a panel discussion.

3. The experts get the information and help the recorder write it up. They then give it to the reporter, who reads over it. Let the groups meet so the reporter has the opportunity to ask questions of his/her group.

4. Have the reporters form a panel discussion. The teacher may moderate or a student may be chosen to do so. Ask the panelists questions designed to compare the strikes. If a panelist has trouble with a question, allow any of the experts to give more information.

5. Close with the questions, "Do we see a pattern in these strikes? Did they all have similar causes? What were they?"

Extensions: Continue your investigations by researching a more current strike, especially one that occurred in your community. Try to get someone involved in a strike to visit the classroom.

Have students make picket signs that relate directly to the strike that they researched. Display the signs.

Labor Dispute Research Sheet

Name of the dispute: _____

Date(s) of the dispute: _____

Name of the company: _____

Name of the labor union: _____

Important characters on the company's side: _____

_____

Important characters on the labor union's side: _____

_____

Governmental officials or agencies involved: _____

Describe the union's motives and actions: _____

_____

_____

_____

Describe the company's motives and actions: _____

_____

_____

_____

Describe the government's involvement: _____

_____

_____

_____

How did the strike end? _____

_____

_____

Daily Writing Activities

Assign an appropriate topic to your class.

Lyddie

1. Describe a machine that you have operated.

2. Imagine that you have moved from the country to a city. What would it be like? What changes would you have to make?

3. Describe the ways that Ezekial and Lyddie are similar. How are they different?

4. Diana helps Lyddie adjust to life at the mill. Describe a favor that someone has done for you.

5. In this section, Lyddie teaches Brigid how to run the looms. Tell about a time you taught someone how to do something. Was it hard to be patient?

6. Describe a time you were sick. Who took care of you?

7. Describe a time you were very lonely. How did you feel? Was there anything that made you feel better?

8. Describe a time that something happened to you that you thought was unfair. How did it make you feel? What did you do?

Breaker

1. On Pat's first day, Chester Cezlak throws rocks at him when he isn't looking. Describe a time when someone was mean to you for no reason. How did you feel?

2. Pat gets mad and says something in anger that later he is sorry he said. Has that ever happened to you? Describe what happened.

3. Michael Kulik is very unhappy because he has lost his wife. Describe a time you lost someone or something.

4. Joanna takes walks because her house is crowded and she likes the quiet of the hills. What is a place that you think is quiet and peaceful? Describe the place.

5. Chester Cezlak has a nickname for Pat: "flea." Do you have a nickname? If you could have one, what would it be? Why would you pick that nickname?

6. Cal has developed a talent for carving. He makes beautiful birds. If you could make something beautiful, what would it be? Describe what you would like to make.

7. In this section, Cal comes home and shares Christmas with the family. Describe your favorite holiday and how you like to celebrate it.

Writing Ideas

The following poems will offer students a number of perspectives on industrialization and how it changed society. The method for introducing each poem is the same—read the poem, discuss it, then offer it as a model for student writing.

- **Walt Whitman and "To a Locomotive in Winter"**

  Read the poem to the class. Discuss the poet's feeling and attitude toward the machine. Does he admire it? How do the students know that? Does it seem interesting/odd to write a poem to a machine? What machine could they write a poem to? Have the students pick one and address a poem to it. Make sure the students directly address the machine in the poem. They could pick anything from the space shuttle to a can opener. Have the students make pictures or get photos of the machine and post their poems.

- **Emily Dickinson and the Train**

  Find the Dickinson poem (number 585) that begins "I like to see it lap the miles." Contrast this poem with Whitman's. Are both admiring? What is Dickinson's attitude toward the train? What does she compare the train to?

- **William Blake and "The Chimney Sweeper" from "Songs of Innocence"** (*There is also a poem by the same name in "Songs of Experience."*)

  Read the poem to the students. Explain that Blake wrote this poem at the time of the Industrial Revolution, when the London sky was darkened by coal fires. Discuss the life of the children as depicted in this poem. Compare it to the lives of the children in the book. Have the students write poems about working children and what their world was like.

- **Carl Sandburg and "Southern Pacific"**

  Read the poem and discuss how it is different from the Whitman poem. How are the two men in the poem different? How are they the same? Does Sandburg favor one over the other? Find other poems about labor/management relations. Write poems about being a laborer or owner during this time period.

- **Lyddie's poem**

  Lyddie makes up a funny poem about Uncle Judah to cheer up Rachel. The poem is much like a limerick. Ask the students to write their own, using either the form in the book or the standard limerick form.

Sources

Walt Whitman in *Leaves of Grass*. Airmont, 1965.

Emily Dickinson in *The Complete Poems of Emily Dickenson*. Little, Brown & Company, 1890.

William Blake in *The Poetry and Prose of William Blake*. Doubleday Anchor, 1970.

Carl Sandburg in *The American Tradition in Literature*. Grossett & Dunlop, 1956.

Dickens at the Mills

Charles Dickens was the most famous novelist of his day in both England and the United States. In 1843 he took an extended trip through the United States, after which he wrote a book called *American Notes*. Here is a quote from the book:

> *They reside in various boarding-houses near at hand. The owners of the mills are particularly careful to allow no person to enter upon the possession of these houses, whose characters have not undergone the most searching and thorough inquiry. Any complaint that is made against them by the boarders, or by anyone else, is fully investigated; and if good ground of complaint be shown to exist against them they are removed, and their occupation is handed over to some more deserving person. There are a few children employed in these factories, but not many. The laws of the State forbid their working more than nine months in the year, and require that they be educated during the other three. For this purpose there are schools in Lowell....*

Pretend you are Lyddie and you are writing to Dickens about that paragraph. With what statements of his would you agree? About what would you tell him he is wrong?

Agree:

_____

_____

_____

_____

_____

_____

Disagree:

_____

_____

_____

_____

_____

_____

Cubing: Group Writing

Help the students to see a familiar object in a different way by having them focus on specific aspects. The exercise will use all the levels in Bloom's Taxonomy.

Materials: The sample plans call for this activity to be used for each book selection. Bring in a tool or object mentioned in each book (e.g., for *Lyddie* a pot, and for *Breaker*, a lump of coal or baseball).

Directions

1. Divide the class into groups of six, then subdivide each group into groups A-F. Ask all the A's to sit together, and so on for each letter.

2. Place the tool in the center of the room, where everyone can see it. Give each child in the lettered group the following task:

   A. This group describes the object, its shapes, textures, colors, etc.

   B. This group compares the object, explaining how it is like and unlike other objects.

   C. This group applies the object, describing all its uses.

   D. This group analyzes the object, breaking it down into its constituent parts.

   E. This group evaluates the object, describing what it is good/not good for.

   F. This group synthesizes the object, describing how it was made, or describing how you could change it to improve it or have it perform different functions.

3. Each student writes a paragraph. Then have the original group meet and share their writing. The group then collaborates on a piece about the object, using ideas from each of the students.

Extension: Another way to use the initial writing is to have the students construct a cube out of cardboard (a good math activity in itself) and paste the six descriptions on the faces.

If the class does three or more cubes, you could involve younger grades by reading the cube to younger students and asking them to match the objects to the descriptions.

Lyddie and Spelling

Lyddie works hard to improve her spelling, and you can see that she does. Here are some of the words she misspells. Write in the correct spelling beside the word:

surprize	_____	babbies	_____
weving	_____	masheens	_____
rom	_____	mistaks	_____
exakly	_____	prevyus	_____

1. What patterns do you see in the mistakes that Lyddie makes?

_____

_____

_____

_____

_____

_____

2. If you were giving Lyddie advice about how to become a better speller, what would you say to her?

_____

_____

_____

_____

_____

_____

On the Railroad

At the end of the book, Lyddie plans to take the train to Oberlin, Ohio, where Oberlin College is located. She might have spent part of her trip on the Atlantic and Great Western Railway, which went to Cleveland, very close to Oberlin. Below you will find a sample train schedule.

Train Schedule

Town	Miles	Morning Mail Train	Morning Express	Night Express
Salamanca	0	5:20 a.m.	10:48 a.m.	10:35 p.m.
Jamestown	35	7:15 a.m.	11:58 a.m.	1:58 p.m.
Corry	61	8:50 a.m.	1:00 p.m.	12:55 a.m.
Saegertown	97	11:27 a.m.		
Meadville	103	11:59 a.m.	2:55 p.m.	2:35 a.m.
Greenville	129	1:26 p.m.	3:55 p.m.	3:37 a.m.
Warren	162	3:15 p.m.	5:06 p.m.	4:49 a.m.
Cleveland	215	5:20 p.m.	7:15 p.m.	7:00 a.m.

1. What town is 97 miles away from Salamanca? _____

2. How long does the mail train take to go from Salamanca to Cleveland? _____

3. The route was 215 miles long. What is the average speed of the mail train? _____

Challenge: Find the average speed of either of the expresses. How much faster do the expresses go?

The Canals of Lowell

Canals were used to bring water to the mills to provide power. More canals were dug as more companies built factories at Lowell. Below is a map of the canals from 1848.

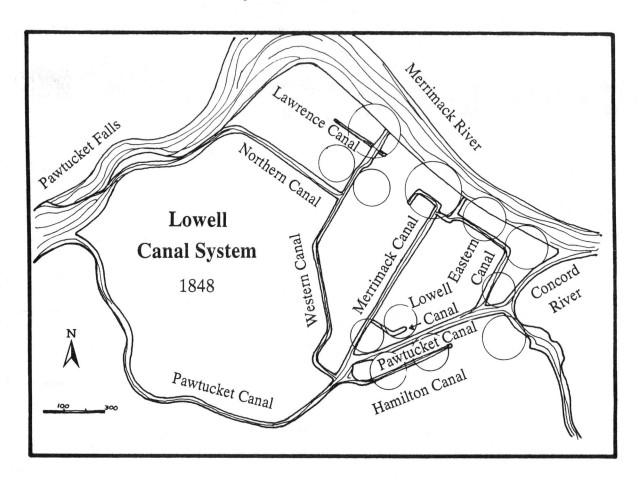

1. Use a ruler to find out the scale. One centimeter equals how many meters? _____

2. Which is the longest canal on the map?_____

3. How long is the Merrimack Canal? _____

Challenge: Use the scale to make an estimate of the area of the town of Lowell inside the Pawtucket Canal and the Merrimack River. Describe how you made your estimate.

_____

_____

Immigration Patterns

Immigrants from all over the world have come to the U.S., and each has in turn supplied cheap labor for U.S. industries. Look at the table and see what patterns you can see in the figures.

Date	Country of Origin			
	Ireland	**Germany**	**Eastern Europe**	**Italy**
1840	46,000	30,000	—	—
1860	221,253	70,000	—	—
1880	60,000	250,000	20,000	15,000
1900	30,000	20,000	350,000*	285,731*

— = fewer than 5,000 immigrants

* These figures are for 1907.

1. What patterns do you see?

   _____

   _____

   _____

   _____

2. What are some reasons people might leave their homes?

   _____

   _____

   _____

   _____

Making the Grade

A grade is a name for a long, slow hill. Because trains pull so much weight they cannot go over steep hills, and even a small grade can be very hard to climb.

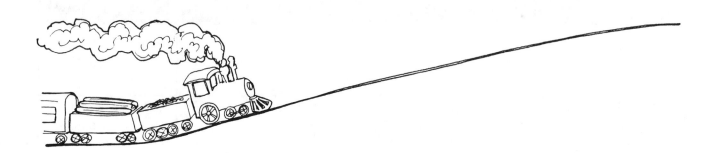

Grades are rated in percent. A 3% grade, for example means that for every 100 feet (30 meters) of distance, the tracks climb 3 feet (.9 meters). You can do some experiments with grades using a ruler, a meterstick, an object, and a spring scale.

Make a grade like the one in this picture:

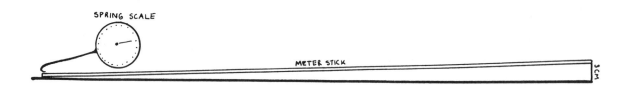

1. Weigh your object. How much does it weigh? _____

2. Attach your object to the scale and pull it up the meterstick. How much does the scale register?

   _____

3. Now make a 4% grade. Pull your object up the meterstick. How much does the scale register?

   _____

4. Now make a 5% grade. Pull your object up the meterstick. How much does the scale register?

   _____

5. What conclusions can you draw from this information?

   _____

Using the Map Unit

Math, geography, and map reading skills will all be used in solving the problems posed in this unit. All the information necessary to answer the questions will be on the map on page 46, but at all times encourage the students to find other maps that might give them more information. The questions are all designed to have more than one solution.

Materials: map on page 46, other maps in almanacs and atlases, a set of encyclopedias if possible

Directions

1. The questions in this unit assume that the students know how to read the legend of a map and are familiar with the idea of scale. Students without a working knowledge of those two concepts will need more guidance through the steps of the problems.

2. Tell the students that the time is about 1865, the end of the Civil War. Briefly go over the map, which shows some of the major transportation routes of the country. It also shows some centers of agricultural products, mining, and manufacturing.

3. There are four questions in the unit. They may be done by students working individually, in pairs, or in groups. Assign one problem each day, and schedule some time at the end of the day to discuss various solutions to the problems. For each question, encourage students to ask questions as subjects for further research.

Example of extending questions for the four pages:

1. How could you find out what St. Louis was like in 1865? How many Germans emigrated to the St. Louis area?

2. Where else in the U.S. are there deposits of iron? Another steel production center was Birmingham, Alabama. How did it become one?

3. Get a map of a city and study it. Make up some questions for classmates to solve.

4. Find population figures for the same states in 1900. (Look in an almanac.) What patterns do you see? How could you explain them?

Map

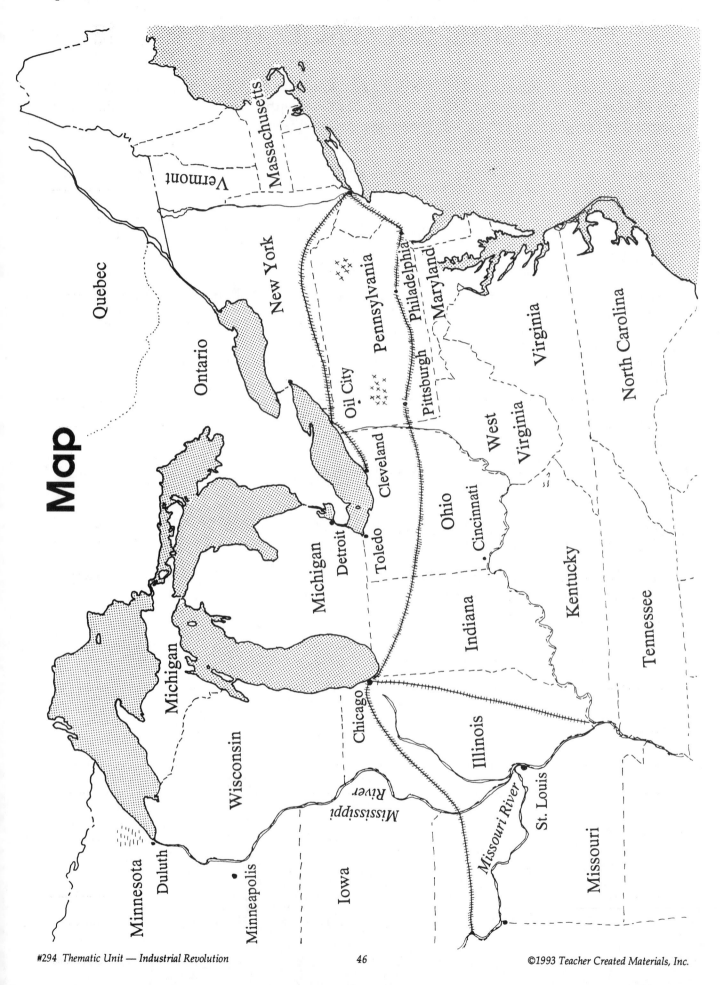

How Uncle Fritz Got To St. Louis

In the 1860's many Germans emigrated to the United States. Fritz was one of them, sailing to New York City and then traveling to St. Louis to join his sister and her family. Find three ways that Uncle Fritz could have made the trip.

Route #1

_____

_____

Route #2

_____

_____

Route #3

_____

_____

Duluth to Pittsburgh

1. Two materials that are necessary for the production of steel are coal and iron ore. Pittsburgh became the place in the U.S. where most of our steel was produced. Why?

2. The largest iron ore deposit in the United States is near Duluth, in Minnesota. Describe two ways that iron ore could be shipped to Pittsburgh.

Route #1

_____

_____

Route #2

_____

_____

3. Which do you think would be the better route? _____

4. How could you find out?

_____

_____

Why Chicago?

Between 1845 and 1870 Chicago grew from a small city to one of the largest in the country. It became a major steel manufacturer and the largest center for meat packing and food processing in the world.

1. Why did it happen in Chicago? Look at the map and write your explanation.

_____

_____

_____

_____

_____

_____

_____

_____

_____

_____

_____

_____

_____

_____

_____

_____

2. Describe what route you would take to go from your city to Chicago.

_____

_____

_____

_____

_____

_____

_____

A New Rail Line

It is 1865. There are many railroad lines east of the Mississippi, and only a few west of the Mississippi. You are advising a railroad company that is interested in building more tracks. Here are some population figures, comparing the populations of selected states in 1850 and 1860. What would your advice to the country be?

	1850 population	1860 population
California	92,597	379,994
Georgia	1,057,286	1,184,109
Maine	583,169	628,279
Minnesota	6,077	172,023
Nebraska	fewer than 5,000	28,841
Oregon	12,093	52,465
Vermont	314,120	315,098

Write your report here. Explain your reasons.

_____

_____

_____

_____

_____

_____

_____

_____

_____

_____

_____

_____

A Time Line of Inventions

Match the invention on the left with its date on the right.

1. First U.S. Locomotive   A. 1901

2. Radio Signals   B. 1879

3. Typewriter   C. 1793

4. Ballpoint Pen   D. 1867

5. Kodak Camera   E. 1939

6. Cotton Gin   F. 1827

7. Electric Washer   G. 1888

8. Helicopter   H. 1830

9. Cash Register   I. 1838

10. Friction Match   J. 1895

Help your teacher make a time line of inventions and post it. Fill in these dates and see how many dates of other inventions you can find. Some possibilities include the invention of the car, the phonograph, the telephone, the computer, and the television.

The TV on the Spot Report

Using a contemporary form to give information about past events will lend an immediacy to the events.

Directions

1. Briefly discuss how events in the 19th and early 20th century were reported.

2. Turn the discussion to safety features in large buildings. What things are in buildings that might protect us against the danger of fire? (Fire escapes, emergency exits, fire extinguishers.) How do students think that these innovations became common?

3. Explain that sometimes laws are passed because of specific events that are so horrible that the whole country becomes concerned. Such an event was the Triangle Fire in New York City in 1911.

4. Divide the students into groups of four: one news anchor, one on-the-scene reporter, one camera person, and one victim to be interviewed. Pass out copies of the bottom of this page and have the camera person read it to the group.

5. The students should write the script together. Give them some time to first write it and then practice their parts.

6. Have the groups perform their reports. Most network news stories last about two minutes. Discuss how much real information can be transmitted in that time. For a variation, you might assign some groups to make a report a year after the fire to be able to discuss the aftermath, after briefly summarizing what happened.

Extension: Any news event during the Industrial Age could be used in this context: the Haymarket Riot, the invention of the lightbulb, and the completing of the Transcontinental Railroad are just a few examples.

The Triangle Fire

The Facts:

The Triangle Shirtwaist Company was located in New York City in the top three floors of a ten-story building, located at the corner of Washington Place and Greene Street in the Greenwich Village section of the lower west side of Manhattan. The blaze killed 146 garment workers, mostly young women. Over 50 people tried to jump from the upper floors of the building to avoid being burned alive. About 20 people survived by using a single 18-inch wide fire escape. It was the only fire escape for the whole building. A few others escaped by jumping to the roof of a neighboring building. The employers had locked many doors to eliminate the danger of pilfering by employees. The people could not use those exits when the fire began. Some people tried to use the elevator shafts. They became trapped there.

A Year Later:

The owners of the company have been tried for their many acknowledged violations of existing fire laws. They were acquitted. A Citizens' Committee of Safety investigated 80 other buildings in the area and found many building with no fire escapes at all, or buildings with obstructed fire exits, barred windows, locked doors, wooden stairways, and unlit stairwells. A new Industrial Code has been enacted by the New York legislature, and other states are considering using this law as a model for their own safety regulations.

In the Boardroom of the Mill

Guiding the class through this scenario will help them understand the processes by which groups of people make decisions. It will also help put the issues surrounding slavery in historical perspective.

Materials: Student should each have a slip of paper (see cards below and on pages 53 and 54) which assigns them the number of shares they own, and their speaking part, if any. Students with no speaking part may agree or disagree with any of the other speakers.

Directions

1. Explain that each student is a shareholder (owns a portion) of the Concord Corporation. They are here today to discuss whether to accept a contract for supplying cloth to make clothes for the slaves in southern plantations.

2. Select a manager. Give the manager the first card below. Have the manager present the facts. (Give this student some advance preparation time.) Distribute the strips below and on pages 53 and 54. Have the chairperson of the board lead a discussion, and then take a vote. Each person votes the number of shares he or she has. The students may vote for, against, or they may abstain. The secretary counts up the votes and declares the winner. The corporation has 5,000 shares; so, if everyone votes, 2,501 or more are needed to win the vote.

3. Give students time afterwards to discuss the reasons for their decisions. Also give the students time to reflect on the fact that in 1830 all the female students and members of minority groups would not have been allowed to be on the board.

Extensions: This exercise is a good springboard for investigations of the beginning of the abolitionist movement, the economic realities of the slave trade, or any other issue where economics and values intersect.

Cards

You are the manager of the mill. Here are the facts that you should present: It is now 1830. Due to a recent depression, the mill has not been doing well financially. There is a demand for cloth to make clothing for African slaves in the South. The cloth is easy to make, because it is not well made. It would be very profitable to begin making it. The finest cloth in the world is still made in England, because they have better technology. It would take a great investment of money to make cloth that would complete with the English. At present, the mill is not making a profit. You are laying off workers, and if the mill continues to not make a profit, the mill might have to close. You own no shares in the mill, so you don't vote.

You are the secretary of the board. Your job is to count the votes after the discussion. Each person casts a number of votes equal to his number of shares. The people who own more of the mill have more power. You own 350 shares.

Cards (cont.)

You are the chairperson of the board. Your job is to lead the discussion. You are a fair person and want both sides to be heard. You own 500 shares.

You are the treasurer of the board. You are in a bad financial position personally, and you really need to make some money. You own 250 shares.

You are the vice-president of the board. Your wife is against slavery and she has convinced you that it is evil. You think making money from slavery would be immoral. You own 450 shares.

You don't like the idea but you think that if this company doesn't make the cloth, somebody else will. You own 100 shares.

You own a dress shop and you owe the bank money. If you don't get the money soon, the bank will take away your business. You own 175 shares.

You are not sure how to vote. You own 200 shares.

You own 100 shares.

You own 25 shares.

You own 50 shares.

You always agree with the vice-president. You own 30 shares.

You don't like the idea, but you owe the treasurer some money. If you vote against him or her, will he/she demand payment? You own 65 shares.

You own 15 shares.

You own 20 shares.

Cards *(cont.)*

You own 600 shares. You are very old and the mill is important to you for support.

You own 250 shares.

You are strongly anti-slavery. You own 50 shares.

You own 115 shares.

You own 250 shares.

You own 190 shares.

You own 85 shares.

You own 115 shares.

You own 95 shares.

You own 215 shares.

You own 125 shares.

You own 250 shares.

You own 160 shares.

You own 70 shares.

You own 100 shares.

The Assembly Line vs. the Cottage Industry

In this activity students will have a basis for comparing the assembly line with the cottage industry mode of production, where one person does the entire job.

Materials: copies of the directions on page 56, a star template for each group of assembly liners and a star template for each individual workperson, paper plates (at least 9 inches/23 cm in diameter), scissors, straws, tape, markers

Directions

1. Divide the class into two parts: half individuals and half factory workers (who in turn are subdivided into four job titles: tracer, cutter, taper, decorator). Explain that industrialization brought with it a form of manufacture called the assembly line, and that they will have a chance to compare the old and new way of making things.

2. Give the individuals the entire set of directions and pass out the materials to them. Give the assembly line workers only the directions for their job and only the materials they will personally need.

3. Give the students time to get completely set up. Have the assembly line workers sit in the order of their jobs. They will do their jobs and then pass the materials to the next person. The individuals will do the whole job.

4. Stop the activity after 30 minutes. Find out who made more star gliders, the assembly line workers or the individuals. Discuss what the job felt like. Is one way of doing things more efficient? Is one way more satisfying? Be sure to go out and try the gliders!

Extension: Save examples of the gliders. Students might use them to practice the redesign step in the culminating activity (page 75) by redesigning the glider.

Directions For Star Glider

1. Trace the star template onto a paper plate. Draw a small circle on the center of the star.

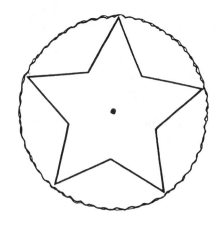

2. Cut out the star. Bore a hole in the center of the star where the mark is.

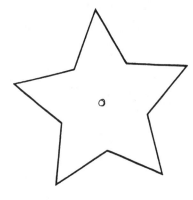

3. Gather four of the cut-out stars and tape them to make one thick star. Make sure the holes in the stars line up. Use a pencil to fix the holes if you need to.

4. Decorate the star. Take a straw and insert it into the hole.

Star Template

Inventor Concentration

Playing this game will help match a drawing of the inventor with some of his/her achievements.

Materials: copies of pages 59-61, backed with construction paper or tagboard, and cut out. The construction paper should all be the same color.

Directions

1. Hand out pages 59-61. Read over the biographical information and answer any questions.

2. Have the students paste the pages on construction paper or tagboard and cut them out. They now each have a set of 18 playing cards, 9 faces and 9 biographies.

3. One player lays out his/her cards face down in a 4 x 5 arrangement. They play a game like concentration, each player turning over 2 cards and trying to make a match of the inventor's picture with his/her biography.

Extension: Students may use these templates to make their own inventor cards and add them to the game.

Name

Picture of Inventor

Name

Picture of Inventor

Inventor Cards

Benjamin Franklin
(1706-1790)

Franklin was not only a famous states-man, he also had a life-long interest in science. He invented the lightning rod to keep houses safe from lightning. He was an early experimenter in electricity (his famous kite experiment), and he built the Franklin stove, a safe, efficient stove which bears his name.

Samuel F. B. Morse
(1791-1872)

Like many inventors, Morse did not begin as one. He spent many years developing his talents as an artist. He was an art teacher at a college and painted portraits and other pictures, but the idea of being able to send messages using electricity began to take up most of his time. He invented the famous Morse Code to translate letters into a series of long and short clicks.

Cyrus McCormick
(1809-1884)

When Cyrus was young, farmers harvested their wheat by hand. It took a long time. McCormick designed a machine that would do it much faster. Other people were trying to do the same thing. Even after McCormick had been successful, he had a hard time selling his machine. More than 10 years after he had first patented his reaper, it finally began to sell.

Inventor Cards *(cont.)*

Elias Howe
(1819-1867)

Howe was born into a large, poor family in Massachusetts. When he was 16, he went to Lowell where he worked in a shop that made cotton machinery. One day he overheard two men discussing how much the world needed a sewing machine. Howe devoted many ideas to making this idea come true. He obtained a patent for his machine in 1846. Like McCormick, he did not become wealthy from his invention for many years.

Elijah McCoy
(1844?-1929)

McCoy's parents escaped from slavery in Kentucky and settled in Canada, as many escaped slaves did. McCoy was apprenticed as a young boy to a mechanical engineer and later went on to invent something called the lubricator cup. Before his invention, machinery often had to be stopped in order to put oil on it. McCoy's invention allowed the machine to be lubricated while it was still on. His name was used for the expression "The Real McCoy."

Alexander Graham Bell
(1847-1922)

Bell was a man of many talents and interests. He was a teacher of the deaf. It was only logical that when he turned to science, his first interest was in the production of sound. After many years, he made a device that would transmit the sound of human speech. He first demonstrated his telephone at the 1876 Philadelphia Exposition. But people did not realize for many years that Bell's invention would change how people all over the world lived.

Inventor Cards *(cont.)*

Thomas Edison
(1847-1931)

Thomas Edison, most famous of inventors, took out patents for more than 1,400 devices. He was not a good student at school but he turned his basement at home into a science lab and worked there every night. As a young man, he worked as a telegraph operator and reporter. He is best known for his invention of the electric lightbulb and the phonograph.

George Washington Carver
(1864-1943)

Carver's parents died soon after he was born. He was raised by the couple who had been his parents' owners before slavery was abolished. They encouraged him to read and to experiment with plants. After he received his college education in Iowa, he taught at Tuskegee Institute and developed almost 500 products from peanuts, sweet potatoes, and pecans.

Garrett Morgan
(1877-1963)

Morgan was born in Paris, Kentucky. He developed a gas mask in 1912. He used it to save 20 workers who were trapped in a tunnel in Cleveland. For his bravery he was awarded a gold medal from the city of Cleveland. A version of his gas mask saved thousands of American lives in World War I. Morgan also developed an early version of the street light.

Philosophical Chairs: The Life Of Carnegie

This exercise gives students a concrete way to evaluate the life of a famous industrialist. It also gives them practice in seeing both sides of an issue.

Materials: Copies of page 63, cut apart and distributed to the students.

Directions

1. Explain that the 19th century produced a number of people who began life in poor or modest circumstances yet went on to gain great wealth. Explain that some people see them as having produced a great deal of wealth for the whole country. Other people see them as having gained their wealth at the expense of most people. One such man was Andrew Carnegie.

2. Begin with a brief, neutral description of his life: He was born to poor parents in Scotland. His father lost his job, so the family moved to the United States. Carnegie worked in a cotton mill at the age of 13. He held many jobs. He accumulated some money and made investments. He began a steel company and ran it for 30 years. He sold it for almost half a billion dollars. At the time, he was the richest man in the U.S.

3. Pose the question, "Did Carnegie do more good or evil during his life?" Have the class chairs set up in a U-shaped arrangement. Students who think he did more good will sit in one row, those who think he did more evil in the other. The bottom row is for those who are unsure. In order to have a good debate, there should be some balance in the numbers in each row. If a vast majority line up in the negative or positive and nobody changes, abandon this question and look for another. Another possibility: "Was the Industrial Revolution a good thing?"

4. Ask the students to make an initial choice, emphasizing that they may change their minds at any time, and that they should show their change of mind by getting up and moving from one row to another. However, only people who are in one of the outside rows can speak.

Extensions: This format can be used to evaluate the life of any of the other industrialists. Give ⅓ of the class the assignment to research negative facts about the topic, ⅓ the assignment to research the positive, and, as a checking mechanism, ⅓ to research both.

The Life of Carnegie *(cont.)*

Evidence in Favor of Andrew Carnegie:

He began life very poor. He worked his way up the ladder by his own efforts.
His company was able to give jobs to many people.
He used the best technology to make the best products he could.
He located his steel mills in a place where the materials he needed were close by.
He gave $60 million dollars to build 2,800 libraries across the country.
He funded an institute that still does educational research today.
He gave $10 million for an institute that would study ways to bring world peace.
Even when he was rich, he still kept working hard.

Evidence Against Andrew Carnegie:

He waited until near the end of his life to give back some of the money he made.
He drove other companies out of business by underselling them.
He employed people at his mill at very low wages.
He employed children at his mills.
He did not publicly oppose a partner in a mill who had some striking workers killed.
He said there were no poor people in the United States at a time when there were.
He ran mills that were unsafe to work in. Many people were injured.
He cut his workers' wages when he was still making a great profit.

Art Ideas

Your Window Frame

Lyddie decorates her window to help her through her work days. Have students construct frames of cardboard and cellophane and/or waxed paper; fill with copied pages from books, artwork, photographs, entries from their journals, cutouts from magazines, lucky charms, souvenirs, postcards, envelopes. Extension: Have students write a description of the window frame and a short artist's bio. Have a show of all the window frames and invite other classes.

"B" Is For Brigid

Lyddie helps Brigid learn her letters using pictures and letters. Gather several examples of alphabet books from the library and show them to the students. Give the students time to make their own alphabet books. See if the students have a younger sibling or friend that they could make the book for. If not, have students give them to students in the kindergarten.

Making A Flag

Have students find pictures of the flags of Vermont and Pennsylvania in an encyclopedia. Students might want to try to pick another state's flag and make a picture of it. Or challenge students to invent their own state and create a flag.

Art From Coal

In the mines, Cal draws pictures of birds. Get some charcoal sticks and challenge students to draw different kinds of birds. Find some examples of birds in painting and pictures as examples.

Another Traffic Signal

Garrett Morgan (page 61) developed an early form of what we all know now as the traffic light. But aren't there many more ways to design traffic lights? Challenge students to create one and make a model or a drawing of their design.

Songs of Labor and Protest

There are numerous sources for recordings of the music of the 19th century as it relates to working people and the labor movement. The following are some sources for songs. Your local or school library may have other sources. The important thing is that having the students listening to or singing some of the songs of working people in the Industrial Revolution will give them a unique perspective about their lives.

Some recordings include:

McNeil, Keith and Rusty. *Working and Union Songs.* (WEM Records, 16230 Van Buren Boulevard, Riverside California 92504.) The address is included in this excellent collection of songs. Some narrative explanation will help the students see these songs in context. A set of two tapes costs $19.95.

Seeger. Pete. *Folkways*, FH 5702. In this concert recording, Pete Seeger shares his comprehensive knowledge of folk music in the United States.

McGee, Bobbie. *Bread and Raises.* (Collector Records, 1604 Arbor View Road, Silver Spring, Maryland 20902.) An excellent set of folk songs with a feminist emphasis.

Spottswood, Richard and Ulman, Rick. *Folk Music in America.* (Recorded Sound Division, Library of Congress, Washington D.C. 20540.) This collection comprises 15 volumes and covers every aspect of folk music. Volume 8, Songs of Labor and Livelihood, is the most relevant volume.

If you play a guitar or piano, there are many songbooks that can supply you with chords and lyrics:

Folksinger's Wordbook. Oak Publication, 1973.

Rise Up Singing. Sing-Out Publication, 1988.

Below are examples of two songs of labor and protest. The first song "We Are Building a Strong Union" was written during a textile strike in 1929. The workers were striking because they only received $10.00 a week, and they had to work 72 hours per week. They were striking because the company tried to increase their shifts. Six workers were shot and killed and 25 others were wounded by state militia. The second song "The Winnsboro Cotton Mill Blues" was written by an unknown millhand in North Carolina.

"We Are Building a Strong Union"
We are building a strong union
We are building a strong union
We are building a strong union
Workers in the mill!
Every member makes us stronger
Every member makes us stronger
Every member makes us stronger
Workers in the mill!
We won't budge until we conquer
We won't budge until we conquer
We won't budge until we conquer
Workers in the mill!
We shall rise and gain our freedom
We shall rise and gain our freedom
We shall rise and gain our freedom
Workers in the mill!

"The Winnsboro Cotton Mill Blues"
Old man Sargent, sitting at the desk
The darned old fool won't give us a rest
He'd take the nickels off a dead man's eyes
To buy Coca Cola and Eskimo pies

I got the blues, I got the blues, I got the Winnsboro cotton mill blues
Lordy, Lordy, spoolin's hard
You know and I know, I don't have to tell
You work for Tom Watson, got to work like the devil
I got the blues, I got the blues, I got the Winnsboro cotton mill blues

When I die, don't bury me at all
Just hang me up on the spool-room wall
Place a knotter in my hand
So I can spool in the Promised Land

When I die, don't bury me deep
Bury me down on 600 Street
Place a bobbin in each hand
So I can doff in the Promised Land

Extension: Often people would take a familiar tune and make up new words for it. For instance, the popular labor song "Solidarity Forever" uses "Battle Hymn of the Republic" for its tune. Students could take a tune they know well and make up a song for it.

Comparing Homemade and Prepared

This activity will compare two ways of cooking.

Materials: box of prepared pancake mix, ingredients of the recipe below, pancake syrup

---

Pancake Recipe (makes 28 four-inch/10 cm pancakes)

3 cups (708 mL) flour

6 tablespoons (90 mL) sugar

3 or 4 eggs

2 to 2 ½ cups (472 to 590 mL) milk

2 teaspoons (10 mL) salt

3 ½ teaspoons (17.5 mL) double-acting baking powder

6 tablespoons (90 mL) melted butter

Sift flour. Resift with salt, sugar and baking powder. Separate eggs, add the yolks to the flour and then beat the whites. Fold them lightly into the batter. Then add the milk and melted butter. Rub some cooking oil on a griddle. Put griddle on a burner at medium heat. Test to see if griddle is heated by sprinkling water onto it. If the water jumps, the griddle is ready. Measure ¼ cup (59 mL) batter for each pancake and pour onto the griddle. When bubbles cover the surface of the pancake, flip it over to the other side. Cook until golden brown. Continue process until you've used all the batter. Add more oil to the griddle if necessary.

Directions

1. Briefly discuss how people cook in *Lyddie*. How is it different from the way we cook now?

2. Make pancakes one day from scratch. Give each child one to taste. The next day make them using a mix to which you only add water.

3. Discuss the two ways of making pancakes. Which is easier? Which pancakes tasted better? You might continue the discussion by estimating how much the two methods cost.

Extension: You might try the same idea with other foods, contrasting prepared foods with the freshly made varieties. Some other possibilities include waffles, French fries, or bread.

Make Your Own Invention

This culminating activity will take groups of students through most of the steps of inventions, from the discovery of a problem to the issue of how to sell it.

Materials: Pages 68-77 reproduced, paper and markers, folders for groups to keep records. Optional materials: if you wish the students to keep an individual record of their group's activities, you will need to supply them with the necessary forms. Also, if you wish to give students time to build models of their inventions, you will need to schedule more sessions and help them get the materials: wood, balsa wood, wire, nails and screws, dowels, and the necessary tools.

Directions

1. The process of invention and discovery can best be understood by experiencing it (as this activity seeks to help students do), and by hearing stories about how other people have made inventions. Page 69 will give you some stories to tell your class. Other books will supply many more.

2. Divide the students into groups of 4 or 5. Tell them that many companies employ design teams to create new ideas and solve problems. Some inventors of the last century, like Edison, used similar teams.

3. Introduce the flow chart on page 68 as one process of invention. Go over each step and explain as necessary.

4. There are seven sessions devoted in the Sample Plans for this activity; however, if students get very involved in design and redesign, do not hesitate to give them more sessions.

5. Each day have a different member of the group be the recorder. Also, give groups a brief review time at the beginning of the session and a brief report to the class at the end of each session. Each student should feel that his/her input is important for the group's work. End the unit with the groups presenting their inventions to an audience.

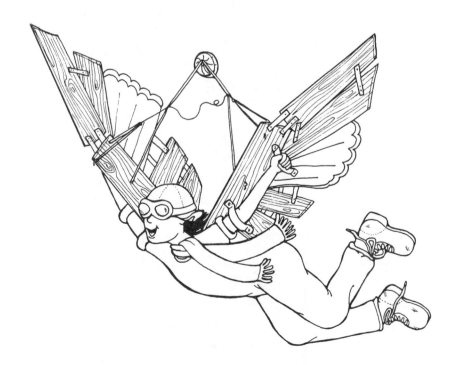

Flow Chart for Inventions

Rules for Brainstorming

1. Accept all ideas, even impractical ones. No criticism.
2. Generate as many ideas as possible.
3. Build on each other's ideas.

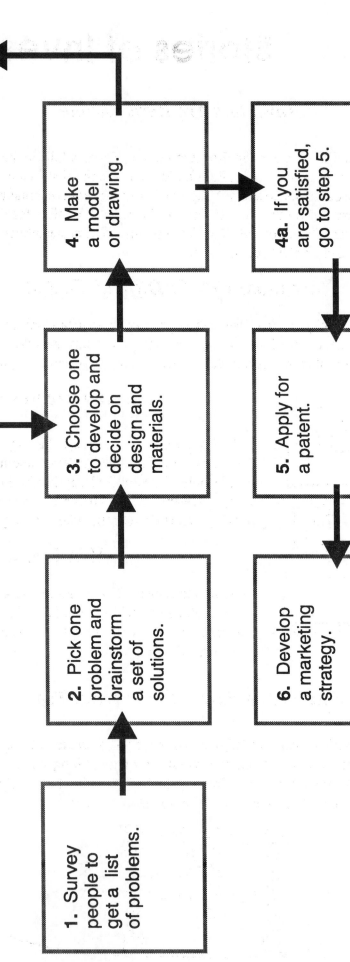

1. Survey people to get a list of problems.

2. Pick one problem and brainstorm a set of solutions.

3. Choose one to develop and decide on design and materials.

4. Make a model or drawing.

4a. If you are satisfied, go to step 5.

4b. If you are dissatisfied, redesign your invention and go back to step 3.

If a redesign does not fix the problem, return to step 2.

5. Apply for a patent.

6. Develop a marketing strategy.

Stories of Inventions

Inventors Are Rarely Alone

Henry Ford did not make the first automobile. Thomas Edison did not make the first electric light. Robert Fulton did not make the first steamboat. Ford was the first car maker to apply the assembly line process to car manufacturing. Edison improved on the electric light, so he made it feasible for the electric light to replace the kerosene lamp. Fulton built the first steamboat that was a practical and financial success.

Inventions Can Be Difficult To Sell

Cyrus McCormick could not sell his new reaper because farmers had no money when they most needed the reaper, right before they harvested their crops. He solved the problem by letting the farmers pay on the installment plan.

Keeping Records Can Be Important

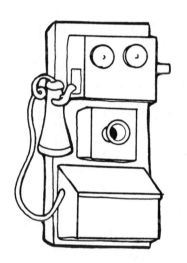

Students who are not used to having writing be a part of every subject may wonder why they need to write about science. Tell them this tale. When Alexander Graham Bell applied for his patent, another man claimed he had made a telephone years before. He was probably correct, but he kept no records of his experiments. Bell, who kept very exact records, was awarded the patent.

Why Inventions Happen

A woman named Bette Graham had a job as a typist. But she was not very good, and kept making mistakes. She invented a kind of quick-drying white paint to fix her own mistakes. Liquid paper! You might know it as White Out or correction fluid.

Failure Is a Part of the Process, Too

Edison and his assistants tried over a thousand substances in the electric light before they found one that would burn for a long time. When Marconi, the inventor of the wireless telegraph, tried his first machine, it could only send a signal across the room. Don't give up!

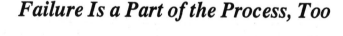

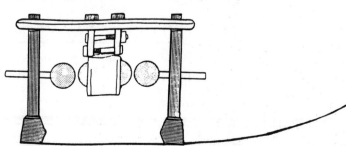

Looking for a Patent

All sorts of devices and machines are patented or are manufactured while the company is waiting for a patent to be approved. Look for things in the classroom that have a patent number or a patent pending on it. For homework, see if you can find some things at home. Write down if the patent has been granted or is pending.

Name of Object	**Patent Number**
_____	_____
_____	_____
_____	_____
_____	_____
_____	_____
_____	_____
_____	_____
_____	_____
_____	_____
_____	_____

Problem Survey

1. Survey people to get a list of problems.

Name of person: _____

1. What things don't work as well as you would like them to work?

   _____

   _____

   _____

2. What is your hardest job at school/work?

   _____

   _____

   _____

3. What is your hardest job at home?

   _____

   _____

   _____

4. What could make your life easier?

   _____

   _____

   _____

Brainstorming

2. Pick one problem and brainstorm a set of solutions

1. Which problem did you pick? _____

2. List the solutions.

_____

_____

_____

_____

_____

_____

_____

_____

_____

_____

_____

_____

_____

_____

_____

_____

_____

_____

_____

Our Invention

3. Choose one to develop and decide on design and materials

1. Which solution did you decide to try? Why?

  _____

  _____

  _____

2. What materials will you use to make your invention?

  _____

  _____

  _____

3. Briefly explain how your invention will work.

  _____

  _____

  _____

  _____

  _____

  _____

  _____

  _____

  _____

  _____

Drawing

4. Make a model or drawing

Make a drawing of your invention. Use a ruler to make your lines straight. Include the dimensions, in centimeters or meters.

Date:_____

Name of draftsperson:_____

Redesign the Invention

4b. Redesign

If you are doing this step, that means that something in the invention does not satisfy you. Here are some ways of asking questions that might help you find out what's wrong.

1. Should you use another material for a part? Should you take one part out and put some other kind of part in?

    _____

    _____

2. Should some part or the whole invention become bigger or smaller?

    _____

    _____

3. Should you rearrange the parts? Should the back be the front? Or should the sides be reversed?

    _____

    _____

4. Does the invention have a part it doesn't need at all? Or is the invention missing a part that it needs?

    _____

    _____

5. Does this invention not meet the need you identified in Step 1? Does it meet another need instead?

    _____

    _____

Patent Application

5. Apply for a patent

Names of group members:

_____

_____

_____

_____

_____

1. Name of invention: _____

2. Describe your invention:

_____

_____

3. How does the invention work, and why is it helpful?

_____

_____

_____

_____

4. Who will use your invention? _____

_____

_____

Submit your model or drawing with your patent application.

How Will We Sell It?

---

6. Develop a marketing strategy

---

1. Who will buy your invention?

   _____

   _____

2. Why will they buy it?

   _____

   _____

3. How will you advertise?

   _____

   _____

4. Make up a product description or a poem that you think will help sell your invention.

   _____

   _____

   _____

   _____

   _____

   _____

   _____

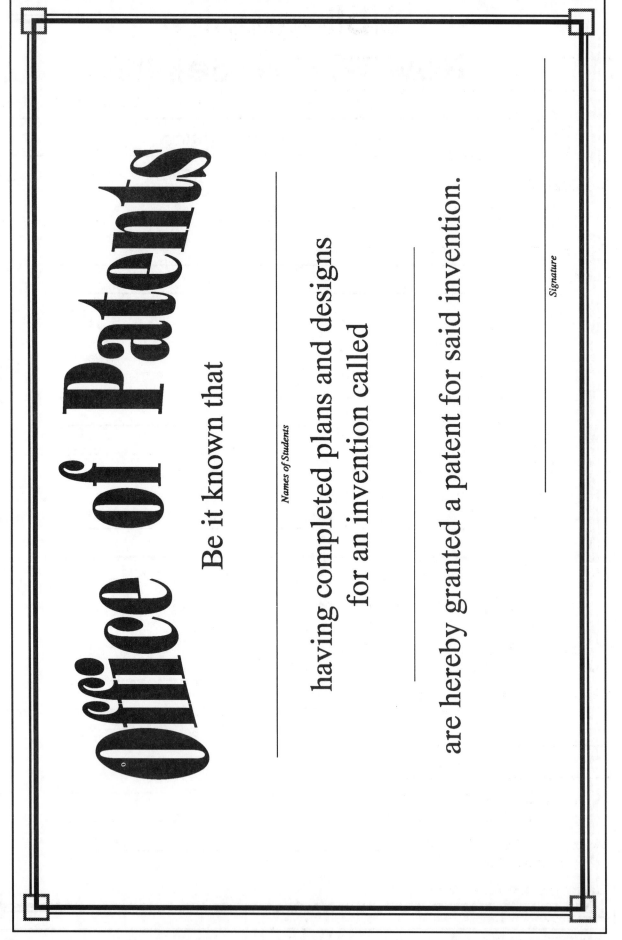

Certificate

Office of Patents

Be it known that

_____

Names of Students

having completed plans and designs
for an invention called

_____

are hereby granted a patent for said invention.

_____

Signature

Bibliography

Books for Teachers

Atlas of American History, 2nd revision. (Charles Scribner's & Son, 1984)

Atlas of the World. (National Geographic, 1981)

Blow, Michael. *Men of Science and Invention*. (American Heritage Publishing Company, Inc., 1960)

Beebe, Lucius. *High Iron*. (Bonanza Books, 1938)

Canedo, Marion. *The Inventive Thinking Curriculum Project*. (U.S. Department of Commerce, Patent and Trademark Office, Washington, D.C. 20231)

Project Excel. (U.S. Department of Commerce, Patent and Trademark Office, Washington, D.C. 20231)

Fisher, Leonard E. *Alphabet Art*. (Four Winds Press, 1978)

Hylander, C.J. *American Inventors*. (Macmillan, 1934)

Kyvig, David and Myron Marty. *Nearby History*. (The American Association for State and Local History, 1982)

Meltzer, Milton. *Bread-and-Roses: The Struggle of American Labor*. (Alfred A. Knopf, 1967)

Morris, Richard and James Woodress. *Voices from America's Past*. (Dutton and Company, 1962)

Weitzman, David. *My Backyard History*. (Little Brown & Company, 1975)

Weymouth, Lally and Milton Glaser. *America in 1876*. (Vintage Books, 1976)

Books for Students

Calkins, Carroll C., ed. *The Story of America*. (Reader's Digest Association, 1975)

Ewing, Norris. *Trains, Tracks & Rails*. (Lane Book Company, 1964)

Graham, Ian. *Inventions*. (Bookwright Press, 1987)

Graham, Rickard. *Canals*. (Bookwright Press, 1988)

Gunston, Bill. *Coal*. (Franklin Watts, 1981)

Hayden, Robert C. *Eight Black American Inventors*. (Addison-Wesley, 1972)

Kraft, Betsy Harvey. *Coal*. (Franklin Watts, 1976)

Murphy, Jim. *Weird & Wacky Inventions*. (Crown Publishers, Inc., 1978)

Pratt, Fletcher. *All About Famous Inventors and their Inventions*. (Random House, 1955)

Silitch, Clarissa, ed. *Yankee's Book of Whatsit's*. (Yankee, Inc. 1975)

Weisberger, Bernard. *Captains of Industry*. (Harper & Row, 1966)

Weiss, Harvey. *How to Be an Inventor*. (Thomas Y. Crowell, 1980)

Weiss, Harvey. *Motors and Engines and How they Work*. (Thomas Y. Crowell, 1969)

Fiction and Poetry

Blos, Joan W. *A Gathering of Days*. (Aladdin Books, 1982)

Paterson, Katherine. *Lyddie*. (Lodestar Books, 1991)

Perez, N.A. *Breaker*. (Houghton-Mifflin, 1988)

Rappaport, Doreen. *Trouble at the Mines*. (Harper, 1987)

Sawyer, Ruth. *Roller Skates*. (Dell, 1936)

Sebastyn, Avida. *Words By Heart*. (Bantam, 1979)

Snyder, Carol. *Ike and Mama and the Black Wedding*. (Putnam, 1979)

Answer Key

Page 9

1. Montpelier
2. Have students check work in encyclopedia.
3. New Hampshire, New York, Massachusetts
4. Quebec
6. 4,393 ft.

Page 12

1. toaster
2. spice grinder
3. corn cobber
4. iron

Page 28

1. Harrisburg

Page 29

1. Dead matter becomes coal by heat and pressure.
2. anthracite, bituminous, sub-bituminous, lignite
3. It adds carbon to the iron.
4. Coal causes pollution.

Page 41

1. Saegertown
2. 12 hours
3. 17.9 per hour

Challenge: Average speed around 25 mph.

Page 42

1. 300 meters
2. Pawtucket canal
3. Around 900 meters

Challenge: You can roughly make a 4cm sq in the map. 1.2 km x 1.2 km= 1.44 sq. km

Page 43

Response should include shift in immigration from Ireland to Eastern Europe and Italy.

Page 47

Answers will vary. Accept appropriate responses.

Page 48

1. Response should include Chicago's close proximity to rail and water transport, as well as abundant agricultural areas.
2. Accept appropriate responses.

Page 49

Response should recommend building toward the west because of the population increases.

Page 50

1. h
2. j
3. d
4. i
5. g
6. c
7. a
8. c
9. b
10. f